Beautiful Packaging

with style and flair

The suggestions contained in this book have been carefully
developed and tested by the author and the publisher. However, no guarantees can be made. The author and/or publisher
and their agents bear no responsibility for any physical or
monetary damages.

© 2005/IMP BV
© for this English edition:
Naumann & Göbel Verlagsgesellschaft mbH, a subsidiary of
VEMAG Verlags- und Medien Aktiengesellschaft, Cologne
www.apollo-intermedia.de

Complete production:
Naumann & Göbel Verlagsgesellschaft mbH, Cologne
Printed in Germany

Beautiful
Packaging

with style and flair

Contents

Wrapping with Tissue Paper

Simple brown kraft paper can be transformed into attractive wrapping paper in a jiffy by the addition of coloured tissue paper cut into different shapes and sizes.

The thinness of tissue paper allows the underlying kraft paper to peer through it to some extent, giving the finished product an in-teresting structure. Overlapping pieces of different coloured tissue paper is also very effective. For an interesting textured effect you can also wad up pieces of tissue paper to form little balls and glue them onto a package that's been wrapped in kraft paper. With so many options, every package will be unique!

Choose tissue paper in contrasting colours. Since it is slightly transparent, it looks pretty when pieces of different tissue papers overlap each other. The torn stripes and pieces of tissue should be irregular, lending the wrapping paper additional flair.

Another way to make use of the thin quality of the tissue paper is by crumpling up smaller pieces, forming little balls and then affixing them to a package already wrapped in plain paper. Cut normal brown kraft paper to the desired size. To attach the tissue paper, it is only necessary to apply a little bit of glue to the outer edges. The tissue will be securely fastened and there won't be any unsightly lumps of glue under the paper. Whether you make stripes, spots, stylised flowers or funny squiggles, it's fun to create wrapping paper that compliments the present and the tastes of the person receiving the gift.

For the finishing touch on a present that will certainly be well received, write congratulations or a greeting on simple white paper and add matching packing twine or ribbon.

A PACKAGE WITH STRIPES AND SQUARES

1 Tear tissue paper of the desired colour in long strips. Tear out small square pieces of tissue in a different colour.

2 Glue the strips and squares of tissue onto the plain wrapping paper. As soon as the glue has dried, wrap up the present.

A PACKAGE DECORATED WITH CIRCLES

1 Wrapping paper can be formed imaginatively using circles of tissue in various hues.

2 Create beautiful colour effects by overlapping the circles when gluing them onto the kraft paper.

A PACKAGE WITH LITTLE PAPER BALLS

Material

- **Plain kraft paper**
- **Tissue paper**
- **Glue**
- **Twine**
- **Scissors**

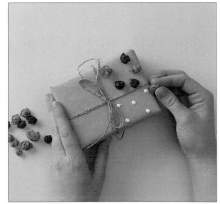

1 Tear two different colours of tissue paper into small pieces and crumple. Roll the crumpled paper between your palms to form small, firm balls.

2 First wrap the present in kraft paper, tie with twine and then glue the little balls on as desired.

Wrapping with Fantasy and Style

*A*ttractive paper and beautiful *gift boxes turn every "little something" into a gift with a very personal touch.*

Unusual packaging often seems complicated, but is actually simple to make. The basic materials you need are card or corrugated card and a craft knife (or other sharp knife). Using the template on

page 48 you can fold and create containers just right to hold all sorts of trifles. The little gift boxes are perfect for small but fine items, such as jewellery. Using raffia, simple ribbons, a stone, a distinctive seed capsule or even snail shells as decoration gives the whole presentation even more flair.

To create this kind of packaging you will need firm, heavy paper. The paper must not give or bend in the wrong place, especially when folding the narrow ends. Beautifully coloured card with a noticeable structure works best. A craft knife, a sharp knife with a fine blade, will easily cut the card. Mark along the template fold lines by carefully perforating sections with the knife.

The rounded end of the knife can be used to add a crease along the perforations. To work cleanly, use a glue stick. Only the long sides of the box are glued; the narrow ends should be folded. For larger or smaller gift boxes, vary the pattern using the enlarging or reducing features of a photocopier.

Material

- **Card or corrugated card**
- **Craft knife**
- **Pencil**
- **Scissors**
- **Wrapping paper**
- **Glue stick**
- **Raffia or simple ribbon**
- **Snail shells and stones**
- **Template on page 48**

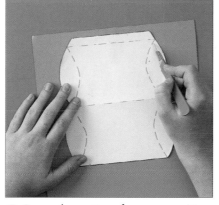

1 Trace the pattern from page 48 onto a piece of card and cut it out. Use a craft knife to perforate the folding lines. The perforations must be visible on the card.

2 Lightly crease the perforations with the handle of the knife to make it easier to fold in the narrow ends later, being careful not to break them.

3 Cut out a piece of wrapping paper, apply glue and attach it to the card. Press on firmly, paying special attention to the edges. If necessary, trim off excess paper.

4 Fold the perforation on the long side and apply glue along the entire outer edge. Glue the two long sides together. Press firmly to set the glue.

5 Fold up the narrow side along the perforations. Place the present inside and fold up the other two flaps to close the box.

6 Finally, tie the raffia or ribbon around the package. To decorate the knot, glue on a seed capsule, a stone or a snail shell.

Silk flowers come in all shapes and sizes. Glue them only along the edge of the lid as a border, or cover the lid completely like a summer field full of colourful silk flowers.

Elegant Boxes in Bloom

*W*ith a little bit of colour and some delicate silk flowers, a plain wooden box can blossom into a flowery gift box, the perfect package for a thoughtful gift.

These delicate boxes are lavishly covered with small flowers and are just the thing for storing beautiful jewellery or other small keepsakes. The wrapping does the trick: a heart-shaped box might hold a pretty gift for Mother's Day or a birthday present for a dear friend. When you are next invited to a party, for example, you could present the host or hostess with a similarly decorated box filled with chocolates.

It's not at all difficult to decorate boxes made of untreated wood. Boxes in a wide variety of shapes and sizes can be found in craft supply stores. Use acrylic paint, which covers well and is easy to mix to paint the box first. Coordinate the colour of the paint with the silk flowers you'll use later. Painting the inside of the box with a lighter shade of the original colour creates a nice contrast.

The paint should be allowed to dry for one or two hours before you glue on the silk flowers. Use glue appropriate for wood and textiles. Apply the glue quite thickly to ensure the flowers are securely attached to the flat surface. These kinds of flowers can be found in a variety of colours in craft supply stores.

The main use for fabric or silk flowers is to decorate wedding dresses and other special occasion gowns. In addition to individual flowers, fabric stores also carry ribbons with silk flower appliqué. Vary the kinds of decorations on the wooden boxes by using other kinds of materials; for example, small gold hearts and ribbons look especially nice when applied close together.

1 Paint the outside and the bottom of the box. Apply the paint with long, even strokes until completely covered. Paint the lid using the same technique.

2 Use a lighter hue of the paint for the inside of the box (simply add some white paint to the original colour). Starting at the top edge, paint down toward the bottom. Finally, paint the inside of the lid.

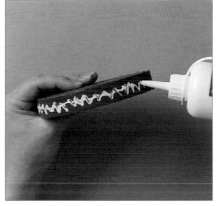

3 First, apply glue in a thick layer to half of the side of the lid. Applying the glue with a zigzag motion assures that the small flowers will be securely glued on.

4 Press the silk flowers firmly to the edge of the lid. Overlap flowers slightly so the surface is completely covered. Apply flowers to the other side of the lid in the same way.

Material

- **Wooden boxes**
- **Silk or fabric flowers**
- **Acrylic paint**
- **Paintbrush**
- **Wood or textile glue**

5 Apply glue to part of the top of the lid. Place the flowers close together, slightly overlapping, to completely cover the wood surface. Let glue dry.

BOX TRIMMED IN ROSES
Lay out fabric roses around the outer edge. Apply glue and press on each rose separately, waiting until completely dry to put the lid back on the box.

Hand-printed wrapping paper is not only an eye-catching way to enclose a gift – it can also be used as the present itself! Simply tie up a roll of the paper with a beautiful ribbon.

Handmade Wrapping Paper

*S*mall tokens, in particular, often take on much greater significance through their presentation. Beautiful packaging often plays an important role here.

With the help of linocut techniques, paper printing is not only a quick and uncomplicated process, but the stamps can be also be re-used again and again. Simple kraft paper becomes individualised wrapping paper.

To store any extra paper, it is best to roll it up with the printed side facing inward. To be able to recognize easily which paper is which without unrolling it, print a tag with the same pattern and tie the tag to the roll.

Transfer the design you have chosen for printing onto a small linoleum plate (or a piece of a plate). Linoleum can be found in craft supply stores or any well-stocked stationary or art supply store. Only a small piece of linoleum is required for the designs shown in this book.

The design can be cut into the linoleum with a special linoleum cutter, called a gouge, although a craft knife works just as well for fine lines. Trace the desired pattern onto the linoleum and cut it out. A cupboard door handle can be glued to the back of the finished linoleum printing plate. This creates a practical printing stamp that is easy to use.

Apply paint to the stamp with a natural or household sponge. A normal paintbrush can also be used. For best results, use non-glossy paper and a small amount of paint to ensure that the contours of the design come through clearly.

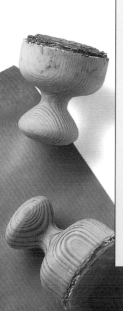

Material

- **Linoleum plates**
- **Natural sponge, common household sponge or paintbrush**
- **Craft paint**
- **Non-glossy kraft paper**
- **Craft knife**
- **Linoleum gouge (optional)**
- **Templates on page 49**

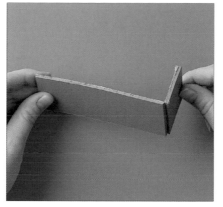

1 Cut out the linoleum plates: cut into the linoleum slightly with the knife, then bend it backward along the line. Finish cutting through the material along the back of the linoleum, using the knife.

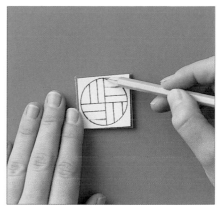

2 Copy the selected design from the templates onto tracing paper. Lay the tracing paper and carbon paper, ink side down, on the linoleum. Trace the motive onto the linoleum plate.

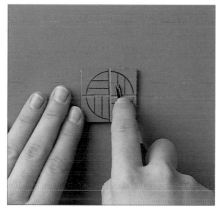

3 Cut out the pattern using a linoleum gouge or craft knife. Don't forget that the pieces you cut out will not be printed.

4 Glue the finished linoleum print onto a piece of wood or an unused cupboard door handle, creating a stamp that can be easily used for printing.

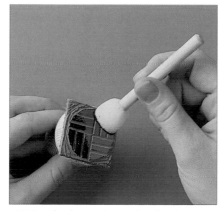

5 Apply the paint to the linoleum stamp with a cut-to-size piece of household sponge or a natural sponge. A paintbrush can also be used.

6 To print the paper, apply only a small amount of paint so that the pattern doesn't run and the design comes out evenly. Practice printing beforehand on a small piece of paper.

Matchboxes can even be padded to give them a truly noble touch. Small shells on unbleached linen create a less complicated, more nature-themed variation.

Fiery Ideas for Matchboxes

*T*hese matches are so charm-
ingly packaged that it will
be a pleasure to take them in
your hands and use them. The
boxes decorated with fabric
and shells are sure to catch
people's eye.

One or more of these fabric-
wrapped matchboxes, imaginatively decorated, can be used as
an attractive table or windowsill
display. When all the matches
have been used you can simply
refill the matchboxes as needed.

In addition, different rectan-
gular shapes can be formed by
using several matchboxes glued
together. Make some of these
practical little "gems" for use at
home or as a small gift.

Matchboxes look much prettier when their rather drab exterior surfaces are covered in fabric. To do this, use either card covered with fabric or finely corrugated card and then glue the heavy paper onto the match-boxes. Suede or Alcantara, a synthetic imitation suede, can also be used. Decorate the fabric-covered boxes with shells, buttons or other suitable objects.

You don't have to dress each individual matchbox: the number of matchboxes can be varied. If you like, you can even create padding for a group of boxes. To do so, simply glue a piece of batting onto the card before covering it with fabric. In this case only the top of the box is padded.

If you have attached several matchboxes to each other, attach a piece of string to the small end of each box by tying a knot inside and outside of the box. Pull on the string to open the matchbox. Instead of string, you can use a fine piece of cord for a more elegant look.

FABRIC-WRAPPED MATCHBOXES

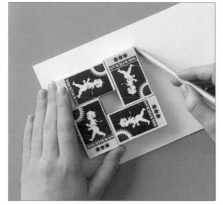

1 Arrange the boxes on the card. Draw lines about 2–3 mm from the edge and cut out 2 equal pieces of card. Cut out fabric pieces that are 1 cm larger than the card forms.

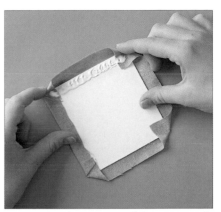

2 Apply glue to one of the pieces of card and press it onto the fabric. Glue the corners and edges down firmly. If needed, use clothes pins to hold down the corners while the glue dries.

3 Glue the fabric-covered card pieces to the top and bottom of the matchboxes. Glue shells on the top.

4 Remove the matches from the boxes and punch a hole in the narrow end. Attach a string by tying a knot both inside and outside.

PADDED MATCHBOXES

1 Cut out a piece of batting the same size as the card pieces and lay it on the fabric. Apply glue to the card and press it on top of the fleece. Glue down the edges firmly.

2 Use a thick needle to sew a button in the middle of the fabric. Glue the thread ends onto the back of the fabric and then glue the padded top onto the matchboxes.

Material

- **Matchboxes**
- **Fabric**
- **Card**
- **Pencil**
- **Shells**
- **Button**
- **Thick needle**
- **Yarn or string**
- **Glue**
- **Scissors or craft knife**
- **Cotton or polyester batting**

Gift bags work well for bottles of wine or other objects with a similar shape. The bottle poking out from the top of the attractive bag is sure to awaken the curiosity of the recipient. Gold and shiny silk ribbons add a touch of luxury to the whole package.

A Bag Full of Gifts

*M*atch the packaging per-fectly to the gift and the occasion by using beautiful paper, ribbons and a variety of decorations.

A luxurious present, such as expensive perfume or jewellery, practically demands an exquisite and handmade presentation. Offer your small gifts in an especially elegant and original way: in a handmade gift bag. Suitable materials for the handle can be chosen from an immense variety of cords, bows and ribbons readily available. You can also decorate the gift bags with feathers or small pictures. An unusual way to fasten the bag is with a loop and button.

Firm paper or thin card is what you will need to put together your own bags, both of which can be found in stationery stores in all colours and qualities. Following the markings on the templates on pages 50–51, fold the paper or card into a bag. If the bag on the template is not large enough, just increase the length or width as necessary.

To get the best results, it is important to crease the paper before you fold it. Crease the fold lines firmly with the back of a knife to prevent the paper from tearing.

Make handles for your bag from just about any kind of cord, string or ribbons. The knots fastening the handles can be decoratively placed on the outside of the bag or hidden from view on the inside. It's especially pretty if the knots are tied using ribbon with smooth ends. If the ribbon tends to fray, hide the knots on the inside. For heavy objects, cover the bottom of the bag with a thick piece of card to give it extra support.

Material

- **Thin card or heavy paper**
- **Thick card**
- **Paper glue**
- **Cloth ribbon**
- **Button**
- **Ruler**
- **Pencil**
- **Scissors**
- **Craft knife**
- **Knife**
- **Hole punch**
- **Templates on pages 50–51**

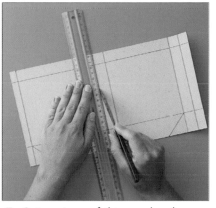

1 Cut a piece of thin card or heavy paper according to the templates with a knife or scissors. Use a ruler to copy all the template markings onto the card and crease them with the back of a knife.

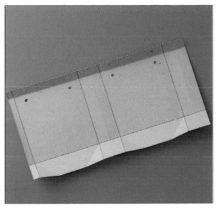

2 Carefully fold the upper edge of the card down. Using a hole punch, follow the markings exactly to place the hole through the doubly folded paper.

3 To make neat corners, fold down all the other edges carefully and precisely. Glue the long sides, briefly pressing them together to ensure the glue holds.

4 Fold and glue the bottom. If desired, cut out a thicker piece of card to strengthen the bottom and place it in the finished bag.

5 Glue the decorations to the bag. Thread the cord, string or ribbons through the prepared holes and carefully tie the knots, inside or outside of the gift bag.

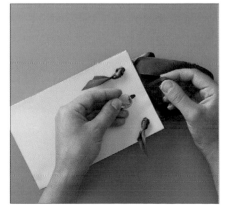

BUTTON FASTENER
Fasten a loop made of ribbon to the button. Punch a hole in each side of the bag and pull the loop through. Hook the loop over the button.

Perfected with Ribbons and Bows

*C*rowned in glory: small packages become festive presents when tied with sumptuous ribbon rosettes – they lend a touch of exclusivity to even the simplest wrapping paper.

Wrapping a present can be a real pleasure, particularly when it marks a special occasion. You can tie magnificent bows out of ribbons of all kinds of colours and patterns. An easy way to create an original look is to tie two bows made from different ribbons next to each other on top of the package. Another option is to choose a patterned bow for paper in a solid colour, or vice versa, to set a pretty accent to the wrapping.

To make a generous bow use wide and relatively firm wrapping ribbon. For bows with more volume, use wider ribbon. Depending on the desired size, a rosette requires between 1.5 and 2.5 metres of ribbon. Because the rosette is tied separately, extra ribbon will be needed to wrap around the package.

Some wide ribbons have wire in their edges to give it greater support. This kind of ribbon is excellent for elongated rosettes. When using wire-edged ribbon to tie round bows, it is not necessary to cut a notch in the ribbon (see step 1 at right).

Presents look especially attractive with two bows placed next to each other, giving the impression of a single large rosette. To increase the effect, use bows made from two contrasting patterns and/or colours. Make the bow a real eye-catcher by wrapping the gift in a solid colour paper. Be sure to select paper and ribbon that coordinate nicely.

- **Firm, wide ribbon (preferably wire-edged)**
- **Thin-guage florist's wire**
- **Scissors**

HOW TO TIE A ROUND DECORATIVE BOW

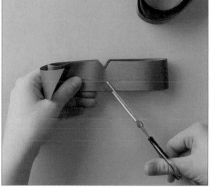

1 Make 5 to 8 loops of ribbon with a width of ca. 15 cm. Measure the centre and use scissors to notch the ribbon there. This is not necessary if the ribbon has wire edges.

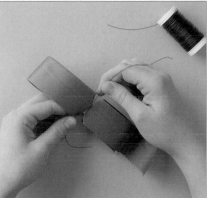

2 Cut a piece of florist's wire 15 cm long. Wrap the wire around at the notched middle of the ribbon a few times and twist the ends firmly together.

3 Pull apart the individual loops with your fingers so that they spring into a rosette. Tease the bow into form.

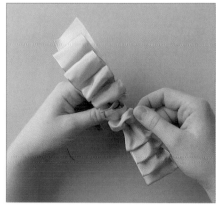

4 Attach the bow to the present. First wrap around the ribbon, then attach the bow using the wire.

HOW TO TIE AN ELONGATED ROSETTE

1 Fold 20 cm of wire-edged ribbon back along itself. Repeat this process, making each loop ca. 1 cm shorter than the previous one. Continue folding in this way.

2 Wrap florist's wire around the centre and twist the ends together. The rosette holds its shape well due to the wire edging.

Gift tags become the crowning touch on any package when each one is as lovingly created as those seen here. A simple printing technique allows you to conjure up attractive patterns on kraft paper in the wink of an eye.

Kraft Paper Charmingly Disguised

*A*ll you need is some plain brown kraft paper, peppy bows, delicate lace and witty accessories like shells, feathers or buttons – and before you know it you'll be creating packages that are out of the ordinary yet inexpensive.

   Give simple paper a new look. To make it even easier to wrap pretty presents, use paper bags, boxes or shipping tubes. Whether you decide to use trimmings in the same colour or a contrasting one, these tips and ideas are sure to turn every gift into the perfect surprise. Also included are suggestions for refining simple brown kraft paper by printing it yourself.

Have we piqued your curiosity to try these techniques for yourself? It is always worthwhile to check what kind of boxes, envelopes, fabrics, papers, strings, ribbons, pearls, buttons, feathers and shells you have are on hand before buying expensive wrapping materials. If you do need to purchase ribbon to make bows, consider buying reusable varieties: broad decorating ribbon (possibly wire-edged) or narrow silk ribbons are easy to untie and use again.

Avoid using glue whenever possible: knotting and tying are preferable. Your presentation will be even more imaginative and can even be given the place of honour as a table centrepiece, as in the example of a box with net and shells.

Shoeboxes offer many possibilities, too. Covered with brown kraft paper (glue would naturally be used here) they provide an ideal platform for decorating. The opening of the box shown here is covered by a piece of burlap wrap used to bind young saplings. For this kind of crafts, it can also be worthwhile to look for supplies in a garden centre.

HOW TO MAKE A SEE-THROUGH SHOEBOX

1 Use a craft knife to cut an opening in the shoebox lid and wrap the box in kraft paper.

2 Cover the window opening with wide burlap wrap and tie down the ends with raffia. Gather a piece of paper into a bow and tie it on.

HOW TO MAKE A BOX WITH NET AND SHELLS

1 Wrap an appropriate size piece of Japanese paper like a sash around the box and attach it with raffia or reeds.

2 Wrap the net around the box as well and pull it tight with the raffia. Use small pieces of twine to tie on the shells and snail shells.

HOW TO MAKE A PAPER BAG WITH BURLAP

1 Attach bamboo chopsticks, feathers and leather strings to a wide piece of burlap. Sew buttons and pearls on the burlap with strands of raffia.

2 Wrap the burlap around a paper bag and tie at the top with a double knot. Fray the ends of the burlap. Tie a large raffia bow underneath the knot.

Material

- **Kraft paper**
- **Shoebox**
- **Paper bag**
- **Decorative materials**
- **Craft knife**
- **Scissors**
- **Glue**

HOW TO PRINT KRAFT PAPER

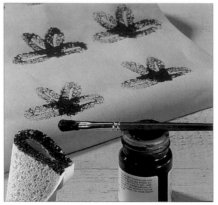

1 Dab the straight edge of a flat household sponge with black acrylic paint and print a herring-bone pattern on kraft paper. Cut a sponge to the appropriate shape if necessary.

2 Bend a flat household sponge in half lengthwise, forming a closed "U" (use a dab of glue to hold it in place if needed) and print a stylised flower pattern on the paper.

3 Using a flat household sponge, cut out circles in various sizes, apply acrylic paint and print on kraft paper.

A Dream in White and Gold

Who would have thought that dreary kraft paper could look so elegant? These example show how the most utilitarian packaging materials can become beautiful creations with just a few, simple steps and accessories. Gold is an ideal addition to elegant white. Together with gossamer bows, delicate lace and extravagant tassels they complete the festive decoration. These wrappings are also easy to open and can be reused, either whole or at least in part.

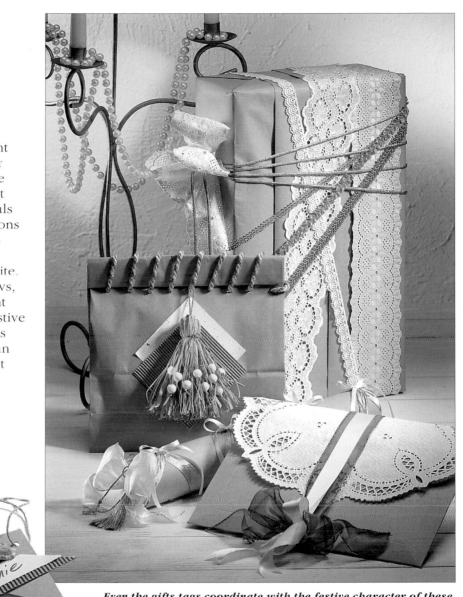

Even the gifts tags coordinate with the festive character of these wrappings. Decorated in white and gold with bows, pearls and more, just like the presents, these gift tags are the icing on the cake!

1 Wrap gold ribbon twice around the packing tube. Glue on the ends and fasten with pins until dry. Gather a wide silk ribbon into a bow and tie with a gold cord. Attach golden tassel.

2 Thread small silk ribbons through the crossing point of the gold ribbon and tie each one into a bow. Glue the large silk bow with tassel on the tube's lid.

3 For the large tassel, tie 30-cm-long raffia strands in the centre with cord. Smooth them down and tie together again just below that. Use a needle to thread pompoms onto the raffia and knot in place.

The proof lies in the details: gift-wrapping made out of unadorned coloured paper fastened with a button creates an unmistakable character, much more so than a simple closure!

Little Presents Sealed with Flair

These simple little bags, which you can easily fold yourself, are transformed into something quite unique and distinctive by their striking closures.

These gift bags are the ideal solution for pretty little trinkets that would be nice to give someone, but until now were perhaps tricky to pack well. Choosing an unusual or even attention-grabbing closure for the bag makes the special surprise just perfect. Once you look more closely at the button display in a fabric shop, a craft and hobby shop or even the sewing box at home, you're sure to find suitable pieces and gain further inspiration for fasteners and embellishments.

Use heavy paper in pretty colours to make these gift bags. The paper you select should be coloured on both sides since the back of the paper will be visible when you fold down the top of the bag. By using heavy paper, the packaging will be durable and stable.

Before gluing the bag together, crease all of the folding lines with the back of a knife to make sure that the corners come out precisely.

Almost any small object you like can be used as a fastener: small wooden figures, beautiful buttons, pieces of wood and bark, shells and much more. The only requirement is that the object be large enough and have one flat side that can be glued to the bag.

For best results, press the fastener firmly in place until the glue has dried. This ensures that the fastener will not slide or fall off.

Material

- **Heavy paper**
- **Tracing paper**
- **Ruler**
- **Scissors or craft knife**
- **Knife for creasing**
- **Glue**
- **Objects for fasteners**
- **Templates on pages 52–53**

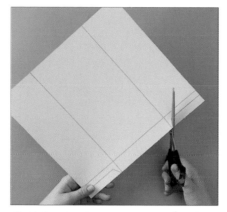

1 Using tracing paper, transfer the pattern from the templates onto brightly coloured paper. Cut out the bag along the marked lines with scissors or a craft knife .

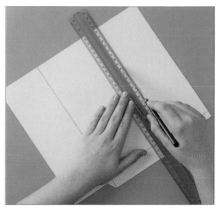

2 First, fold each marking once and then crease the folds (if necessary) with the back of a knife before gluing the appropriate places.

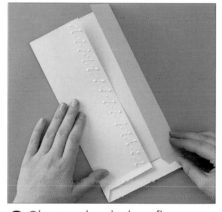

3 Glue together the long flaps on the back of the bag. To ensure that the edges are firmly attached, hold them together with a clothes-pin while drying.

4 Glue the bottom of the bag firmly. Fold the flap with glue applied on it toward the back of the bag and clip together with a clothespin until the glue is dry.

5 Put the sweets or present in the bag. Fold the top of the bag down toward the front, pre-creasing the fold line. Fold the edge straight or at an angle, as you please.

6 To finish, glue the selected fastener firmly over the folded edge. The object used might refer to the recipient or to the gift itself.

Paper in delicate pastel colours combined with dried flowers and crepe paper in matching hues create an enchanting presentation. Handmade tassels of household twine provide additional accents.

Wrapping Paper "Au Naturel"

*W*hether for birthdays, anniversaries or as a thank-you, there are many reasons for that special little something. Wrapped in natural materials, the packaging has an attraction all its own.

With a little time and imagination you can produce these distinctive wrappings made out of inexpensive materials. Kraft paper and twine are wonderfully transformed when combined with small bunches of dried flowers and grass. Plait raffia into neat ribbons or use frayed twine to tie bows. In addition, the packages can be varied by decorating them with eucalyptus, leaves or sticks of cinnamon.

Create individual wrapping variations out of a range of different materials. Simple kraft paper can be nicely enhanced with ribbons and bows made from twine or cord. Make beautiful ribbons out of leftover wool or cotton yarn, or decorate your package with small figures cut out of felt.

Decorating with small bouquets put together from different kinds of plants adds a special charm. For example, you might use large seed capsules such as those from the eucalyptus tree, small pine-cones or twigs bearing rosehips. Attach them to the package with cloth ribbon or glue. Flexible grasses or grain stalks are also quite suitable as decorations. Shells, preferably with holes, work well tied on with raffia ribbon.

Tie up the packages with a piece of rope or plaited raffia. Apply the finishing touches to the decoration with handmade tassels made of string – you can experiment with different colour combinations and thicknesses to achieve the desired effect.

HOW TO CREATE A SPECIAL GIFT-WRAPPING

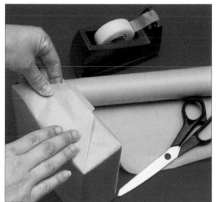

1 Cut brown kraft paper to size and wrap the present. Cut off extra paper at the corners, fold the paper carefully and attach it under the box with adhesive tape.

2 Tie together three long strands of raffia at one end. Pin the knot on a stable pad and braid the raffia together. Use six to nine raffia strands for a thickly braided ribbon.

3 When the raffia is braided, knot the strands at the other end. Wrap the braid around package. Fasten on the underside or tie off with a bow.

4 Bind the dried flowers into little bouquets, with the long-stemmed flowers on one side. Fasten with tape, concealing it under the braid.

HOW TO MAKE A TASSLE OUT OF STRING

1 Cut a 7 x 15 cm piece of card to size. Using two strings of different colours, wind them around the card 10 times (20 times for a thicker tassel).

2 Tie together the loops on one side of the card. Cut through the loops at the other side. Tie off the tassel 2 cm from the top.

Perfumed soaps in a variety of eye-catching packages: cellophane works well with small and playful soap forms, while corrugated card and string does the trick for square soaps.

Fragrant Soaps Delightfully Packed

*I*t is not difficult to decoratively adorn some pretty and fragrant soaps with dried roses, flower petals and shells for use in your own bathroom or as a present for someone else.

Fine soaps can be found pressed into a tremendous variety of forms, in every colour and in fun shapes. The soaps look very striking when gathered into a piece of tulle or cellophane, or wrapped with corrugated card, which is tied together with ribbon or rough twine.

Make extra soap packets in advance to always have a little present on hand. In addition, it is nice to hang a little tulle bag in the linen cupboard or bath.

Perfumed soaps in a wide assortment of shapes and colours can be found in gift shops and department stores. To package them appealingly, however, is an art. The soaps can be embellished in a variety of ways. Let the decorative materials you have on hand serve as your inspiration.

If you want to wrap the soaps romantically in tulle, include some dried rosebuds and a few small shells. Gather the tulle into a little bag, fill it with the soaps, rosebuds and shells, and tie it together with a coordinating coloured ribbon.

Natural materials are particularly well-suited for decorating and packing these gifts. For example, you might place several soaps in a small bowl filled with wood shavings. Wood shavings can be found in pet stores.

Square soaps can be wrapped up most effectively in corrugated cardboard. Tied with simple packing twine, this attractive present gets a clean look in the true sense of the word.

Material

- **Small soaps**
- **Dried rosebuds**
- **Shells**
- **Small dish**
- **Wood shavings**
- **Tulle**
- **Cellophane**
- **Corrugated card**
- **Wide ribbon**
- **Twine**
- **Scissors**

HOW TO MAKE ROMANTIC TULLE SACHETS

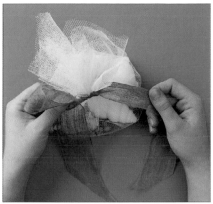

1 Cut out a piece of tulle to size. Lay the soaps, dried rose buds and a few pretty shells on the tulle.

2 Gather the ends of the tulle to form a small bag and close it with a piece of wide ribbon. Tie a small bow.

HOW TO GIFT-WRAP SOAP DISHES

1 Fill an appropriate dish two-thirds full with wood shavings. Arrange different shaped soaps on top.

2 Cut out a piece of cellophane to size. Place the dish on the cellophane, gather the ends around it and tie together with a ribbon.

HOW TO WRAP SOAP IN CORRUGATED CARD

1 Cut a piece of coloured corrugated card large enough to wrap once around the soap. The card should be slightly narrower than the soap.

2 Wrap the card around the soap. Tie with a rough piece of twine, giving the soap the look of a small packet. Fasten securely with a knot.

Gift boxes like these are a beautiful alternative to pack small presents attractively. Cellophane or other transparent material placed behind the opening encourages curiosity.

Decorative Boxes with a View

*D*ecorative cartons with a *peephole cannot help but awaken curiosity about their contents! The geometric opening in the lid barely allows a peek inside.*

Gifts are packed expressively and conveniently in these cunning cartons. Choose different geometric shapes from the templates on pages 54–57 for the little window openings on the lids. For a nice effect you can glue a narrow-guage mesh behind the window, or simply leave it open. A patterned fabric used to prevent inquiring eyes from peering in looks equally effective and increases the suspense while the gift is being unpacked.

With a handmade box, you always have the advantage of being able to coordinate its colour with that of the present it holds. A sturdy gift box can be readily made from thick card.

After cutting the card according to the pattern given on pages 54–57, prepare the fold by cutting just slightly along the folding lines with a craft knife. The cardboard can then be folded effortlessly. With thinner card you need only crease the lines with the back of a table knife.

The packaging looks particularly original when you cut little peepholes into the lid and cover them from behind with cellophane or small-meshed net.

Alternatively, using beautiful fabrics that are colour-coordinated with the giftwrap works just as well. The carton also looks very striking if the opening is not covered, encouraging guesses about its contents.

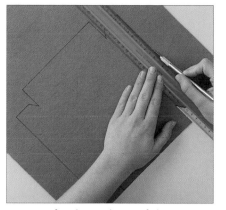

1 Transfer the outlines of the template to a piece of card 1 mm thick. Cut out the carton form with a craft knife, using a ruler to be exact.

2 Select a pattern for the window openings from the templates, use tracing paper to transfer it to the card lid and cut out the form carefully.

3 Score the card along the folding lines with the craft knife. If you are using thinner card, crease the lines with the back of a table knife.

4 Cut out a piece of gold net or material with a comparable structure about 1 cm larger than the window in the lid. You can use the window template to cut out the net.

Material

- **Card, 1 mm thick**
- **Pencil**
- **Ruler**
- **Craft knife**
- **Scissors**
- **Glue**
- **Clothes pins**
- **Netting, fabric, cellophane or paper**
- **Templates on pages 54–57**

5 Carefully apply glue on the inside of the lid around the window opening. Glue on the net so that the right side faces out of the window.

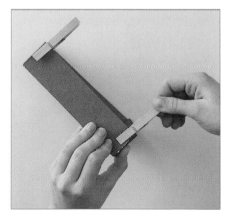

6 Apply adhesive to the sides of the lid and glue together. Use clothes pins to hold the glued pieces together while drying. Fold and glue the box in the same manner.

Combine a variety of papers: the pattern on the box lid is produced by peeling apart pasted papers; the one on the box and the folder, by using a comb technique.

Stripes, Checks, Waves and Dots: Paste Paper!

*P*aste patterns are a beautiful method of decorating paper which can then be used for any number of original packing possibilities. Making the paper is not at all complicated – and the results are all the more impressive.

The name says it all: paste paper is paper which has been covered with a layer of coloured paste in which you then draw lines with the help of notched trowels or combs to create varied patterns. There are also other methods to decorate with paste paper: you can stamp it with corks, crumple the paper or put two sheets of paper together and then pull them apart.

CREATING STRIPED PATTERNS

Smooth, firm papers (70 to 115 g/sqm) such as fine stationary or drawing paper are well-suited for creating paste paper. To make the paste, stir 4 heaping tablespoons of wheat starch into a little water, being careful to avoid lumps.

Bring 1 litre (1 quart) of water to the boil in a pot, then slowly add the starch, stirring continuously. Bring to the boil again and then let the mixture cool. Colour the paste by adding some acrylic paint and stirring well.

You will need several wide and narrow flat brushes as well as different notched trowels to make the patterns. A plastic trowel with flat notches or a large, rounded off galvanised comb as well as a plastic kitchen spatula can work very well. The points of the notches can be shortened with scissors to make the desired notch width.

The paper must be prepared before spreading the paste. Paper expands when it comes into contact with moisture and becomes wavy. Wet both sides of the paper with a little water before you begin so that it will lie flat when the paste is applied.

1 Cut plastic trowels to the desired size. Trim trowels with pointed teeth by drawing a straight line with a ruler and marker and cutting the teeth off with scissors.

2 Mix 4 tablespoons wheat starch with a little bit of water in a small bowl. Bring 1 litre (1 quart) water to the boil and slowly stir in the starch. Bring mixture to the boil and let cool.

3 Wet both sides of the paper to be decorated with a sponge. Mix a portion of the paste with acrylic paint and apply evenly to the paper with a flat brush.

4 Draw diagonal lines with a wide-toothed comb, pressing lightly, from the upper left to the lower right corner. Line up the outer tooth of the comb with a previously made line to continue the pattern unbroken.

5 Continue the patterns over the entire sheet of paper, making lines from the upper right corner to the lower left corner. Let dry and iron on the back if needed.

CHECKERBOARD PATTERN
Cut trowel to desired size. Draw horizontal and vertical squares in a row. Alternate the pattern in the following rows.

Material

- **Wheat starch**
- **Sponge**
- **Wide and narrow flat brushes**
- **Light coloured paper (fine stationary or drawing paper)**
- **Different notched trowels or combs**
- **Scissors**
- **Corks**
- **Rubber gloves**
- **Acrylic paint**

CREATING SPIRAL PATTERNS

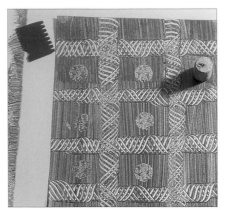

1 Holding the trowel vertically, draw narrow, tightly spaced wavy lines from top to bottom on the pasted paper. Make the rows about 5 cm apart from each other.

2 Turn the sheet of paper 90 degrees and again draw rows of wavy lines from top to bottom. With a knife, cut off a cork evenly and use it to make a stamp in the centre of each square.

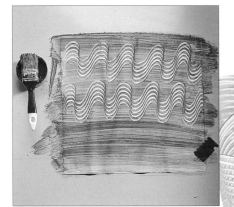

CREATING WAVY PATTERNS

Wet the sheet of paper and then brush on coloured paste. Holding the trowel vertically, draw large wavy lines on the paper.

Idea

This same technique can be used to create multi-coloured paper. To do this, make three lines of coloured paste next to each other, each the width of a brush and in a single colour. Then you can work with the paste to get the pattern you want. Instead of using trowels to draw lines and circles, try finger painting or stamping the paste-coated paper.

Simple Methods for Stunning Structures

Perhaps the easiest way to make patterns on paper is simply to crumple up the paper spread with paste. Through this technique, some of the paint flows into the folds and the effect of the pattern is almost three-dimensional. Straighten out the paper, let it dry and iron it from the reverse side.

Another technique is to place two sheets of pasted paper together and then carefully pull them apart from each other. This method results in patterns that resemble the structure of ferns. This pattern also can form the background for further processing of the paper later with a brush or trowel.

1 First, apply paste paint evenly to two sheets of paper. Gently press the painted sides together and then peel off the top sheet.

Whether you use it to cover books, to glue on boxes and photograph albums or to wrap special gifts: handmade paper with beautiful patterns and structures always creates a lasting effect.

2 You can use these sheets as the background for additional patterns: for example, draw evenly spaced stripes with a paintbrush, or create a comb pattern with a trowel on top of the stripes.

CRUMPLED PAPER TECHNIQUE

Wear rubber gloves for this! Apply a generous amount of coloured paste to the paper, then wad it up from the outside to the inside. Then carefully straighten the paper and let dry.

These square boxes lend themselves especially well to combinations of colours. The champagne bottle wrap below is made from glossy card and a golden doily.

Boxes in Extravagant Forms

*E*ven tiny presents make a big splash packed in these original boxes. The boxes can be made for a wide range of occasions and can even be coordinated with the gift.

Whether in the form of a bag or a pyramid or a cube, each box is an original decorated with beautiful handmade border trim and ribbons. The containers are so stable that they can be used again for storing small things. Sturdy card, coloured corrugated card and glossy card are ideal raw materials for the pretty packaging. Try experimenting with other kinds, as well, of course: the most important thing is that the card be relatively firm.

All the patterns on the template sheets can be changed to any size you desire. However, keep in mind that boxes will be less stable as their dimensions increase.

The most important tools for this project are a ruler, a pencil, a creasing tool and a craft knife.

First, use tracing paper and pencil to transfer the templates to the back of the card. Cut along the solid lines, then crease well along the dotted lines with the blade of a table knife. The card can be folded easily in these places later. Apart from glue and perhaps double-sided adhesive tape, all that's needed now is matching cord, ribbon or raffia for fastening the box shut.

For the pyramid-shaped box you'll need a little coloured tissue paper as well: the gift should be loosely wrapped in tissue paper and placed in the box. Then the sides are folded up and tied with ribbons so that the tissue paper peeks out at the four sides.

Whether monochrome and elegant or multi-coloured and fun, you determined the style of these boxes with the decorations you select.

How to Make a Box for a Bottle

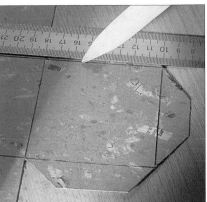

1 First, use a pencil and ruler to trace the template onto the back of the card in the desired size. In the photo the lines have been traced in felt-tip pen for better visibility.

2 Cut along the outer edge of the pattern using a ruler and craft knife to keep the lines precise. Crease the dotted lines with the creasing tool. This makes the cardboard be easier to fold later.

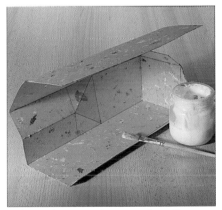

3 Transfer the markings for the holes and cut them out with a hole punch. Fold up the card, pressing in the side edges.

4 To glue together, apply adhesive to the bottom and glue one side flap after the other to the bottom until the bottle box has 4 sides.

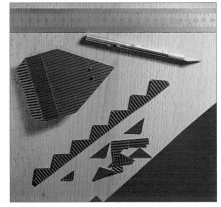

5 For the corrugated card fastener, lightly score the card along the dotted lines with the knife. Punch holes and glue to the back from the inside. Attach decorations.

6 Thread a double strand of raffia through both holes from the inside. Thread the raffia through the holes in the fastening flap and tie it in a bow.

Material

- **Different sorts of stiff card**
- **Ruler**
- **Pencil**
- **Creasing tool**
- **Double-sided adhesive tape**
- **White glue**
- **Brush**
- **Craft knife**
- **Ribbons, cords and raffia**
- **Golden doily**
- **Hole punch**
- **Scissors**
- **Templates on pages 58–59**

HOW TO MAKE A PYRAMID BOX

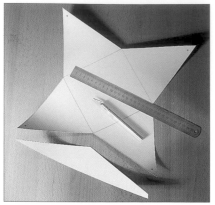

1 Using tracing paper and pencil, copy the template on the back of copper-coloured card, for example, and cut out with a craft knife.

2 Punch a hole into each upper corner of the 4 side pieces and crease the dotted lines with the creasing tool. Cut out a piece of golden doily and attach it with glue.

3 Loosely wrap the gift in tissue paper and place it in the box. Fold up the sides. Thread a matching ribbon through the holes, pull together gently and tie with a bow.

Gift Boxes with Elegant Decor

It is not just the neat way these boxes close that is so attractive, but also the closures themselves. Cut from card of contrasting colours, for example silver and copper, it is possible to create these wonderful boxes by hand. The corners of the closure are rounded off. Strengthen the sides of larger boxes simply by gluing a golden paper ornament over the edges. The closure flaps can also be decorated this way.

Ornaments punched or stamped out of paper can be found in stationary stores with a large paper assortment. Motives cut out of doilies work just as well.

When changing the size of the pattern on the template sheet, don't forget that the bottom of this particular box must always be a perfect square. You can shorten or lengthen the sides as needed: the surface area of the closure flaps should always be half of the area of the box's base.

Splendid in gold, silver and copper: no matter how small the gift is – it will always be well received in these elegant boxes. The colours of the card can be combined in new ways over and over again.

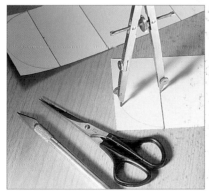

1 Cut two pieces of card from each colour. To round off the corners, use a compass placed in the middle of a side's upper fold line, draw a semicircle and cut off the corners.

2 Go over the fold lines firmly with the creasing tool or table knife. Pre-fold both strips of card. Lay the bottom pieces over each other and press together with double-sided adhesive tape.

3 Fold the box together. Cut out golden paper motifs and glue them onto the corners. Glue motifs to the middle of the fastening flap as desired.

Instead of using wrapping paper, you can cut newspaper in strips and use it to create witty packaging. A ribbon made of bright raffia is the icing on the cake. Spruce up the matt finish of the checkerboard wrapping with a few strips of glossy paper.

Cleverly Woven Wrapping Paper

*E*xtravagant packaging can be made from a collection of used wrapping paper or from the strips left over when cutting gift wrap to size.

No matter how beautiful the wrapping paper is, it is usually thrown away after just one use. If you cut it into strips, however, and interweave it with diverse materials – such as patterned or solid paper, metallic or opaque cellophane – you will have a new and original covering for your gifts. Wrap a matching ribbon around the present and add a tag made out of one of the wrapping scraps. Such cunningly packed surprises bring an additional portion of joy.

Make your woven packaging out of two differently patterned gift wrap. Before you begin, measure the carton that is to be wrapped exactly so that the finished woven paper is large enough to cover it. Measure the long upper edge of the box for the horizontal line and the narrow edge for the vertical line.

The length of the horizontal strips, which will be the weft when weaving, is calculated by adding twice the height of the box and the horizontal measure. Calculate the length of the vertical stripes, which will later form the warp strips, by doubling the vertical measure and adding it to two times the box height. Add 1 cm to the total.

Using a sharp craft knife, cut the strips to size: 1.3 cm wide and as long as you need them to be.

Prepare as many vertical stripes (warp threads) as necessary for the individual strips placed next to each other to equal the length of a horizontal strip. You will need enough horizontal strips (weft threads) to cover the length of a vertical strip. If you need to piece strips together to achieve the required length, tape the strips with adhesive tape on the back.

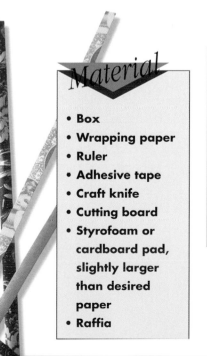

Material

- **Box**
- **Wrapping paper**
- **Ruler**
- **Adhesive tape**
- **Craft knife**
- **Cutting board**
- **Styrofoam or cardboard pad, slightly larger than desired paper**
- **Raffia**

1 Measure the box to be wrapped. Calculate the length of the horizontal and vertical strips and select fitting papers accordingly. Use a ruler and knife to cut the paper into even strips 1.3 cm wide.

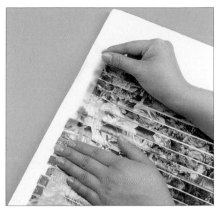

2 Lay enough vertical strips very close together on the styrofoam or cardboard pad so that they equal the length of a horizontal strip. Fasten the ends to the pad with adhesive tape.

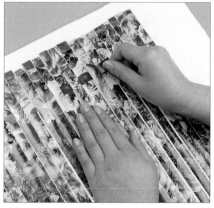

3 Weave the first horizontal strip starting just below the taped ends. Begin by weaving over the first strip, under the second, over the third, continuing in this manner until the end of the strip.

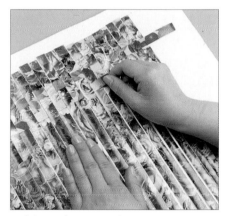

4 Start the second strip in reverse order, beginning under the first strip, over the second, etc. The horizontal strips should be woven closely together, with their side edges touching.

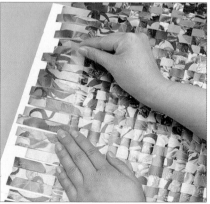

5 Continue weaving in this manner, keeping the rows even, straight and close together. Tape down the finished woven paper ends, remove the sheet from the pad and lay it on a cutting board.

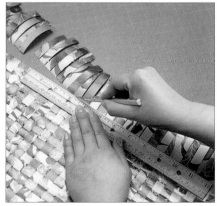

6 Place the ruler along the outside edge of the tape. Remove overhanging ends with a craft knife. Wrap the paper around the box, being careful not to pull too tight. Wrap and tie a bow with raffia.

Lemons don't have to be sour! Not only citrus lovers will be happy at the sight of these lemons. The bowl or basket is an additional gift.
The delicate flowers below reveal their secret only on closer inspection: the bills are real and the flowers forged.

Gifts of Money – Always a Good Catch

Often desired and always welcome: gifts of money help dreams come true, whether large or small. Instead of the usual envelope, these gifts can be presented in much more ingenious ways.

Anyone who lands this fish comes home with a real whopper! The money it bears is surely no mere fisherman's tale; there's more to the story than meets the eye. You determine the value of the fish with the type and size of its scales: it's up to the fisherman to decide how big "the one that got away" should be.

Additional accessories like fishing net, a piece of sisal and shells make the catch perfect.

How to Make a Coin-filled Fish

Two fish bodies are cut out of photo mounting paper, and then the two parts are glued together at the end. This prevents the coins from slipping through and helps the fish maintain its form even if it gets a little "over-weight".

There is a design suggested on the template on pages 60–61, but the fish can of course be represented by many other types: you might consider making a slim trout, a quick pike or a silvery minnow.

You can also vary the colour and make fish from silvery-grey, turquoise, green or red mounting paper.

For a thoughtful house warming gift, simply wrap the stuffed fish loosely in a little aluminium foil – it should still be peeking out – and place it in an appropriately large ovenproof baking dish. Garnish the dish with a few sprigs of fresh rosemary or a little bouquet garni.

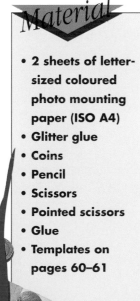

Material

- **2 sheets of letter-sized coloured photo mounting paper (ISO A4)**
- **Glitter glue**
- **Coins**
- **Pencil**
- **Scissors**
- **Pointed scissors**
- **Glue**
- **Templates on pages 60–61**

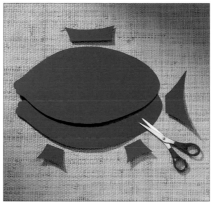

1 Copy the fish from the templates onto the mounting paper using tracing paper. Trace the body twice, each fin once, and cut the pieces out carefully.

2 With a pencil, draw the eye, mouth and gills onto one of the fish bodies. For the scales, trace three-fourths of the way around one of the coins with a pencil.

3 Using small, pointed scissors to cut out the individual scales carefully along the pencil lines. Bend the scales up a little if you like.

4 Carefully apply glitter glue to the pencilled contours on the fish's head. Also edge the individual scales and decorate the fins. Allow the glitter glue to dry thoroughly.

5 Glue the fins onto the decorated fish body. For the backside, apply glue to the edge of the second fish body and press on. The scales should be kept free of glue!

6 Carefully bend all of the scales open a little bit once again. Slide the coins under each scale so that a part of the edge remains visible.

HOW TO TWIST PAPER FLOWERS

1 Cut pieces 3–6 cm wide from a pack of crepe paper, depending on what size flower you desire. In sections, stretch the cut edge of the crepe paper tightly over a blunt knitting needle or similar object.

2 With the stretched edge facing up, continually twist the crepe paper strip into a flower. Twist the flowers tightly or a little more opulently, as you like. Hold the flower in place with gold wire.

If you would like to embellish fruits like apples, lemons, oranges, pineapple or others with leaves made from bank-notes, you can simply attach them with pins. For a small flower arrangement, however, it is best to fasten the folded-money leaves with strong florist's wire so that they can be inserted in floral arranging foam.

3 First, halve the bills lengthwise. Then fold the corners into the centre once or twice. Cut out leaves from construction paper, also folding lengthwise, and attach to the bills. You may wrap them with wire.

Idea

In case your gift is intended to be financial support for someone making a journey abroad, why not give money in the currency of the country they'll be visiting? Perhaps you can think of a typical symbol for the vacation destination that can be included in the gift-wrapping.

Mice, Mice Everywhere Mice!

Seeing is believing: there really are white mice cheerfully scampering over bread and cheese! They are made from paper and, unlike their living counterparts, have a particularly pleasant quality: the soft little tails are wrapped around carefully folded banknotes.

No one could fail to be enthusiastic at the sight of this kind of mouse – keep the cat away and let the mice play!

These comical little animals can be presented to anyone, young or old, in many different ways. Pose the mice individually or in a group, under a cupboard or behind the curtains, between books, on top of tinned goods or very simply under a cheese globe. Or maybe you have a better idea!

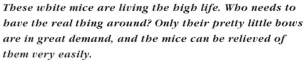

These white mice are living the high life. Who needs to have the real thing around? Only their pretty little bows are in great demand, and the mice can be relieved of them very easily.

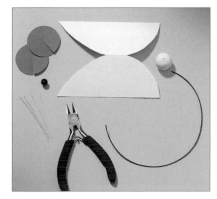

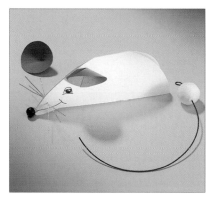

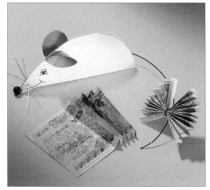

1 Materials: Photo mounting paper (for the body), construction paper (ears), silver wire (whiskers), a wooden bead for the nose, wire and a cotton ball for the tail.

2 Draw a mouse face. Glue nose, ears and tail onto the body. Push the whiskers through a small hole, attach securely and spread apart.

3 Fold the banknotes into little zigzag folds, like a fan. Indent the folds in the centre and wrap around once with the mouse tail.

Decorate the fabric bottle covers with an application if you don't want to make an opening for the label to peer through. A sewn gift tag adds a lovely personal touch.

A Perfect Fit for Good Spirits

*B*eautiful fabric covers adorn elegant bottles of wine and make less aristocratic drops more presentable, whether as an original gift idea with a nametag or for your own use at home.

Dress the bottles in beautifully coloured and patterned high-neck slipcovers. Decorate the cloth covers with an application, or make a cut-out opening to highlight the label of the bottle effectively.

Coordinate the fabric with your table decoration: whether rustic or festive, there's a matching fabric for every occasion. As a small present for your hosts, as well, a bottle packed in this way will certainly be well received!

These beautiful fabric covers are perfectly tailored for wine bottles. Therefore measure the fabric pieces carefully before cutting. For a standard-size wine bottle, make a cover from two rectangles with the following measurements: 24 x 27.5 cm and 14 x 27.5 cm as well as a fabric circle with a diameter of 9.5 cm. The cover can also be sewn from a single piece of fabric instead. For this variation cut a rectangle 36 x 27.5 cm in size. Fold down 6 cm from the top edge and hem the fabric 1 cm from that edge.

Stiffer fabrics often work best. Thinner fabrics may be doubled, or you can apply interfacing to the reverse side to give the material more strength. Measure the placement of the label on the bottle and transfer the measurements to the fabric in order to cut it precisely. Hem the edges of this window with zigzag stitch.

Sew a gift tag made of doubled fabric lined with interfacing and hem around the edges and the opening. Thread the tag on a string or ribbon and tie it in a bow.

Material

- **Fabric**
- **Ruler or tape measure**
- **Pencil**
- **Sewing pins**
- **Thread**
- **Needle**
- **Scissors**
- **Sewing machine**

1 Cut two fabric rectangles 24 x 27.5 cm and 14 x 27.5 cm and a fabric circle with a diameter of 9.5 cm for the bottom of the bottle. Measure the label position and transfer to the larger piece of fabric.

2 Cut the opening for the label and carefully hem the edges all round with zigzag stitch. Take care that the opening has exactly the same shape and size as the label on the bottle.

3 Then place the fabric with the opening on top of the smaller fabric piece, with the right sides together. Pin and sew the pieces together along the top edge of the larger rectangle.

4 Fold the sewn pieces lengthwise with right sides together. Pin the layers together along the open edge and then sew the long sides of the cover together.

5 Pin the fabric circle for the bottom from underneath, right sides together, and sew it securely in place. Be careful to avoid creating folds while sewing.

6 Fold the fabric of the top edge of the cover toward the inside, and sew it on securely with a hem stitch. Turn the cover right side out, put the bottle inside it, and tie with a pretty cord or ribbon.

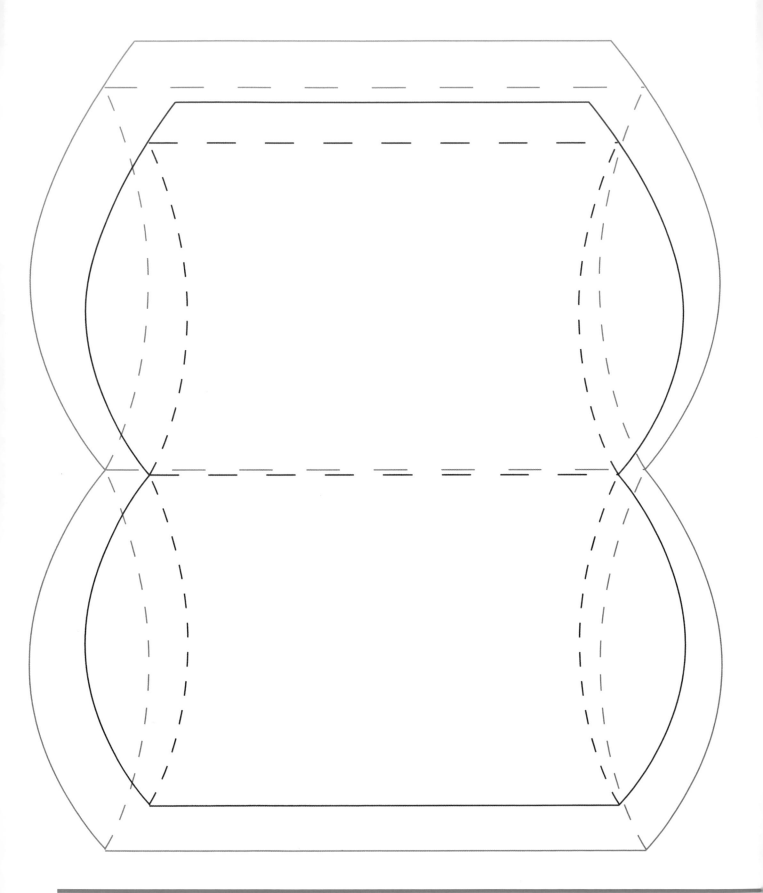

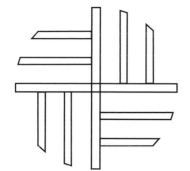
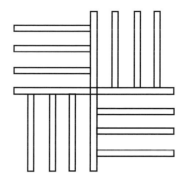
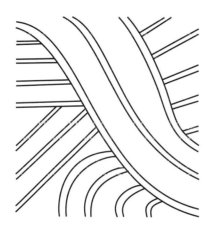
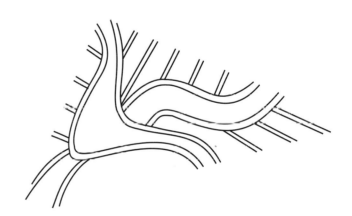
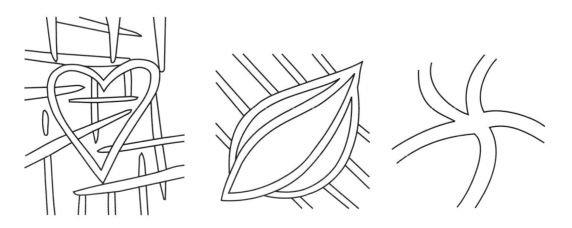

JOIN HERE

Ⓐ

Ⓑ

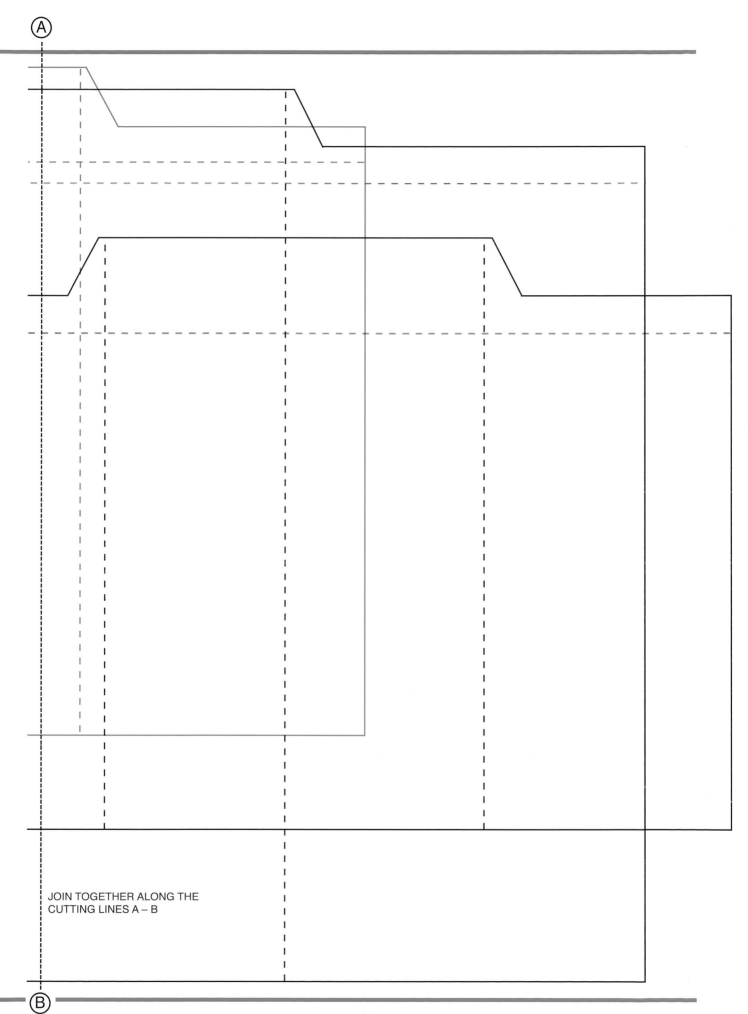

Ⓐ

Ⓑ

JOIN TOGETHER ALONG THE
CUTTING LINES A – B

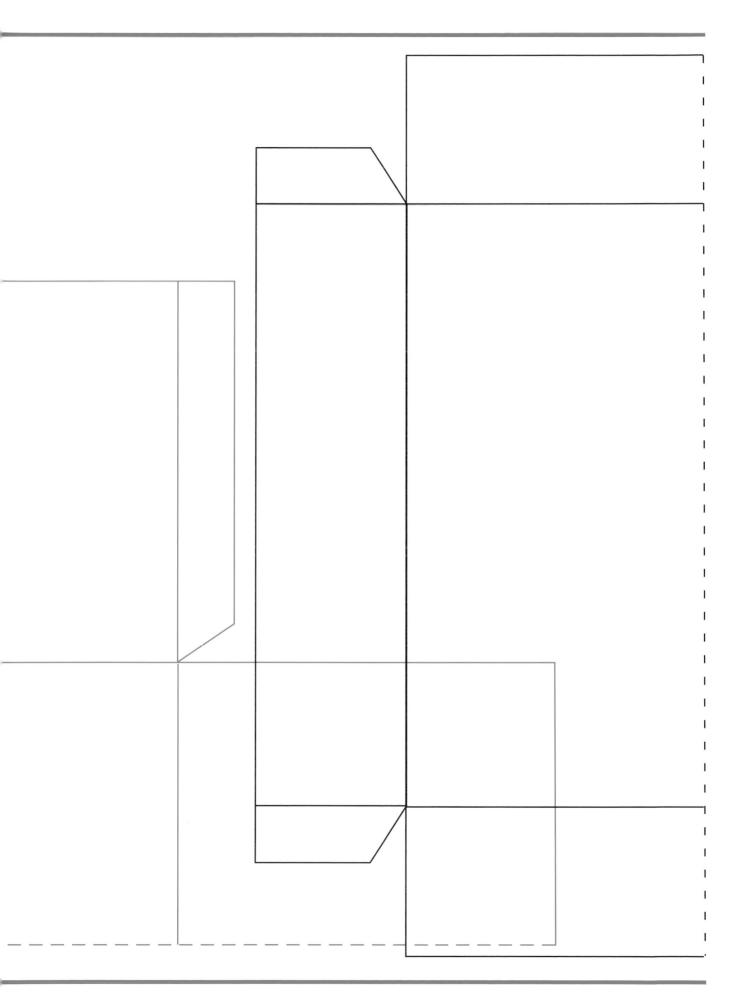

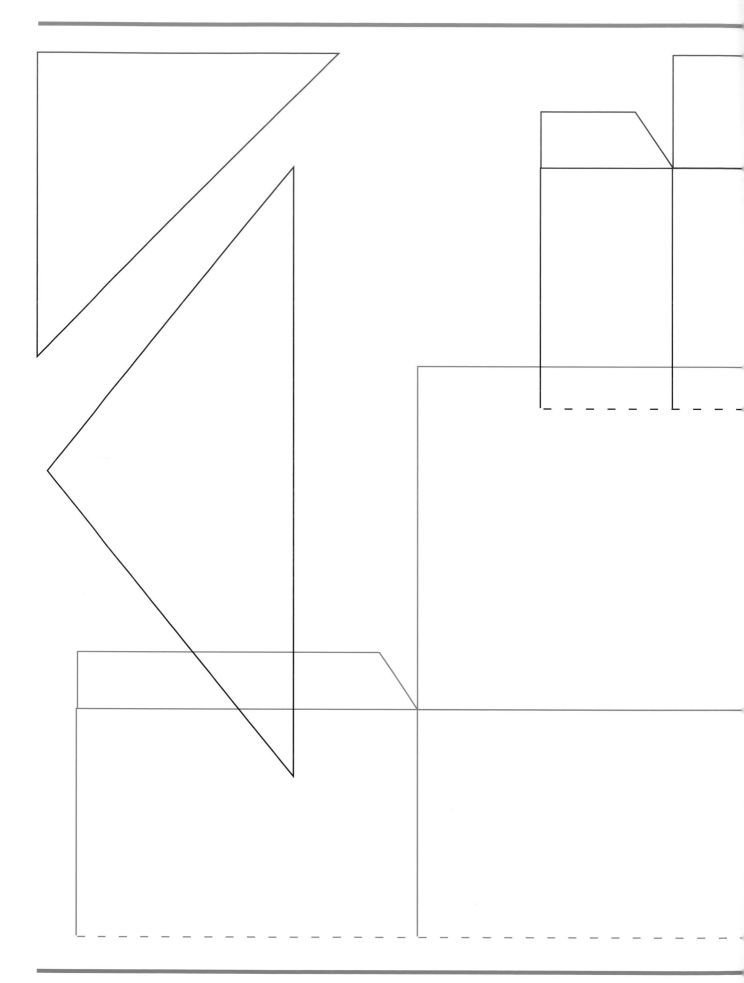

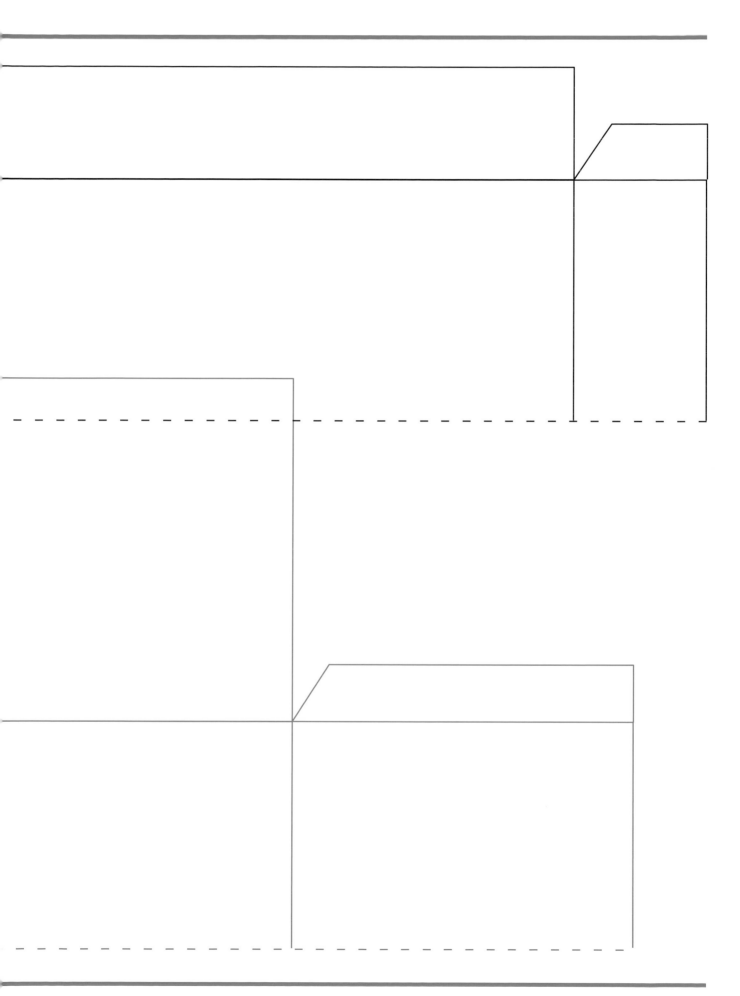

ALL SHAPES CAN BE
ENLARGED OR REDUCED
AS NEEDED

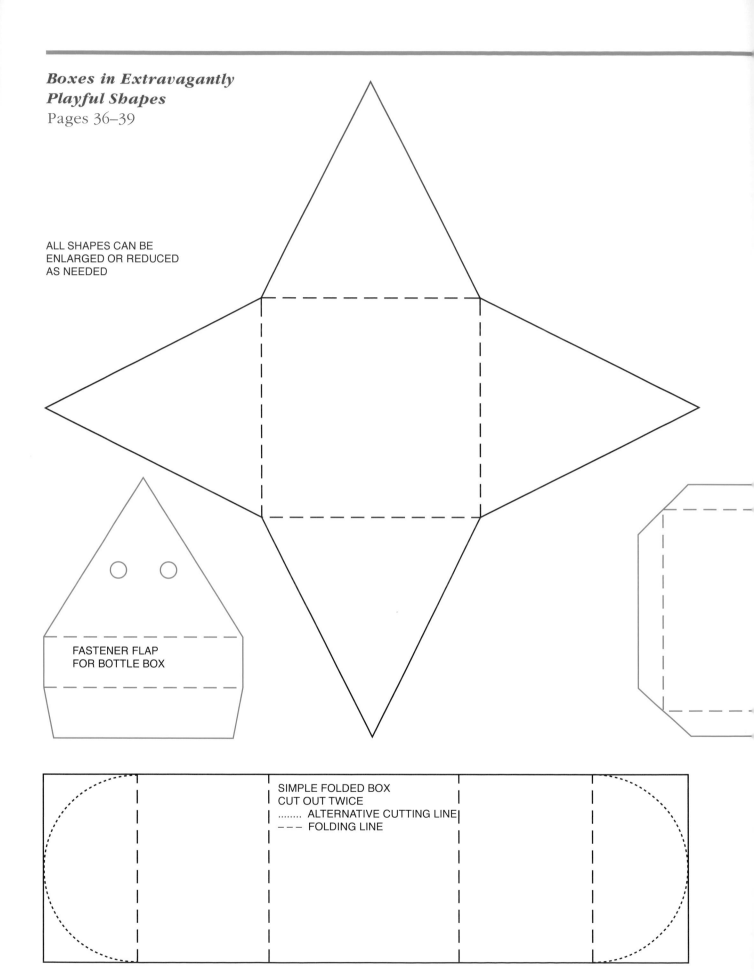

FASTENER FLAP
FOR BOTTLE BOX

SIMPLE FOLDED BOX
CUT OUT TWICE
.... ALTERNATIVE CUTTING LINE
– – – FOLDING LINE

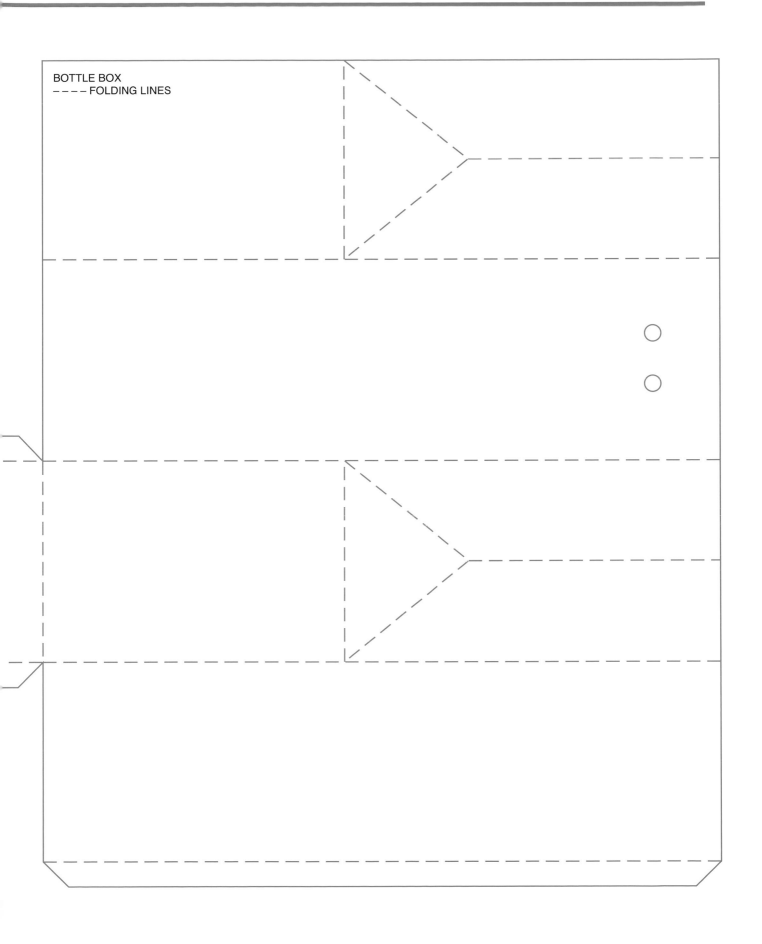

BOTTLE BOX
– – – – FOLDING LINES

TAIL FIN

BACK AND
STOMACH FINS

6

8

10

12

14

16

18

20

24

26

28

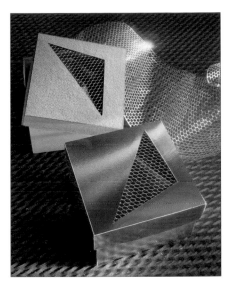

30

32

36

40

42

46